First World War
and Army of Occupation
War Diary
France, Belgium and Germany

59 DIVISION
177 Infantry Brigade
Prince Albert's (Somerset Light Infantry)
11th Battalion
6 March 1918 - 31 August 1919

WO95/3023/6

The Naval & Military Press Ltd
www.nmarchive.com
Published in association with The National Archives

Published by

The Naval & Military Press Ltd

Unit 10 Ridgewood Industrial Park,

Uckfield, East Sussex,

TN22 5QE England

Tel: +44 (0) 1825 749494

www.naval-military-press.com

www.nmarchive.com

This diary has been reprinted in facsimile from the original. Any imperfections are inevitably reproduced and the quality may fall short of modern type and cartographic standards.

© Crown Copyright
Images reproduced by permission of The National Archives, London, England, 2015.

Contents

Document type	Place/Title	Date From	Date To
Heading	WO95/3023/7 11 Battalion Somerset Layout Infantry		
Heading	59th Division 177th Infy Bde 110 Bn Som. Lt. Infy May 1918-Aug 1919. From U.K		
War Diary	Wrentham Suffolk	06/03/1918	06/03/1918
War Diary	Enham Lawn	06/03/1918	06/03/1918
War Diary	Esworth	06/03/1918	06/03/1918
War Diary	Dover	07/05/1918	07/05/1918
War Diary	Calais	07/05/1918	10/05/1918
War Diary	St. Omer	10/05/1918	10/05/1918
War Diary	Brias	10/05/1918	10/05/1918
War Diary	Brias	11/05/1918	11/05/1918
War Diary	Vielfort.	11/05/1918	30/05/1918
War Diary	Vielfort Wood.	31/05/1918	09/06/1918
War Diary	Olhain Wood	09/06/1918	09/06/1918
War Diary	Vielfort Wood	10/06/1918	16/06/1918
War Diary	Huchel	16/06/1918	17/06/1918
War Diary	Sains-Lez-Pernes	17/06/1918	24/06/1918
War Diary	Lhires Delette	24/06/1918	28/06/1918
War Diary	Audingthun	29/06/1918	10/07/1918
War Diary	Ruisseauville	10/07/1918	25/07/1918
War Diary	Bellacourt	26/07/1918	03/08/1918
War Diary	Trenches	03/08/1918	09/08/1918
War Diary	Barly	10/08/1918	16/08/1918
War Diary	Bellacourt	17/08/1918	20/08/1918
War Diary	Trenches	21/08/1918	23/08/1918
War Diary	Saulty	24/08/1918	24/08/1918
War Diary	Mazingham	25/08/1918	26/08/1918
War Diary	Rodecque	27/08/1918	27/08/1918
War Diary	Trenches	28/08/1918	30/08/1918
War Diary	Epinette	31/08/1918	01/09/1918
War Diary	Trenches	02/09/1918	03/09/1918
War Diary	St. Venant	04/09/1918	05/09/1918
War Diary	Epinette	06/09/1918	07/09/1918
War Diary	Pont Riquel	08/09/1918	13/09/1918
War Diary	Trenches	14/09/1918	22/09/1918
War Diary	Bout Deville.	23/09/1918	01/10/1918
War Diary	Charter House Post	02/10/1918	03/10/1918
War Diary	Trenches	04/10/1918	10/10/1918
War Diary	Fleurbaix	11/10/1918	16/10/1918
War Diary	Bois Grenier	17/10/1918	17/10/1918
War Diary	Perenchies	18/10/1918	18/10/1918
War Diary	Marquette	18/10/1918	18/10/1918
War Diary	Monsen Bareul	19/10/1918	19/10/1918
War Diary	Lhemponpont	20/10/1918	20/10/1918
War Diary	Willems	21/10/1918	22/10/1918
War Diary	Front Line	23/10/1918	26/10/1918
War Diary	Hullans	27/10/1918	30/10/1918
War Diary	Front Line	31/10/1918	31/10/1918
War Diary	Esquelmes	01/11/1918	06/11/1918
War Diary	Hulans	06/11/1918	08/11/1918

War Diary	Toufflers	08/11/1918	10/11/1918
War Diary	Pecq	11/11/1918	15/11/1918
War Diary	Chereng	16/11/1918	16/11/1918
War Diary	Seclin	17/11/1918	05/12/1918
War Diary	Noeux Les Mines	05/12/1918	08/12/1918
War Diary	Noeux Les Mines	09/12/1918	15/12/1918
War Diary	Noeux-Les-Mines	16/12/1918	31/12/1918
War Diary	Abancourt	15/01/1919	31/01/1919
War Diary	Blargies Abancourt Area	01/02/1919	07/03/1919
War Diary	Calais	08/03/1919	08/03/1919
War Diary	Coulogne Calais.	09/03/1919	06/08/1919
War Diary	Beaumarais Calais	07/08/1919	31/08/1919
Miscellaneous	Territorial Force Association County Of Somerset.		
Miscellaneous	Short History Of The 11th Somerset Light Infantry.		
Miscellaneous	11th Somerset Light Infantry.	02/11/1919	02/11/1919

WO95/3023/27

1 Battalion Somerset Light Infantry

59TH DIVISION
177TH INFY BDE

11th BN SOM. LT. INFY
MAY 1918 - AUG 1919.

FROM UK

WAR DIARY
or
INTELLIGENCE SUMMARY

Army Form C. 2118.

Place	Date	Hour	Summary of Events and Information	Remarks and references to Appendices
DOVER	7.5.18	7.50	1/2 of A Coy went with 1 M.G. and 3 men reported to an R.T.O. at 9.30 a.m.	
		11.0 a.m.	The population turned in billets and was merry hearty, and full inspection was held	
		1.0	One Mess Cart with M.P. kitchen, as casualty Evans "Osys" Tufnel	
		6.15 p.m.	The Battalion Parade turned out adjutant at 6/6/...	
		5.30	The O.C. Employment Station Officer and 8 runners reported to C. Embarkation Officer	
		6.0	The Battalion entrained. All rank were issued with life belts, and 6 Officers placed in charge of Officers. Swedes were issued to platoon, and also the platoon. O.D. Company were in charge of	
			All M.P. The Baggage Parties. The M.O. Went ashore approved "Baggs" Officer. This was sent M.P. in rations that no Representatives Captn 7/2 B. Standards an appointed	21/5
			Billetting Officer to the wife + Baggage to wait the train	
		7.40	The Boat was left Emb. Quay/arriving at Calais at 11.25. Weather roll "coming over" of the minor or not	
		8.0	ZEEBRUGGE Weather fine. Calm	
		9.20	Arrived at CALAIS and disembarked	
		10.30	Entrained No.6 Rest Camp (Taint)	
		11.30	All Ranks less Officers received and meal all did 2 P.G men	
		1 p.m.		
CALAIS	8.6.18	9.30	The Battalion paraded and moved 8 Platoons to BEAUMARIE Camp. First all were paraded through gun armoury then pressed to tents. The time 37 p.m. The Kitchen was not	21/5

WAR DIARY
or
INTELLIGENCE SUMMARY.
(Erase heading not required.)

Army Form C. 2118.

Place	Date	Hour	Summary of Events and Information	Remarks and references to Appendices
CALAIS	8.5.18	3.30	O.C. C.O. held a meeting of the officers	
		10.30	Men not assigned any duties had all kinds of intelligence	
	9.5.18	12.55	Field airship passed the camp and was very trying, bombs dropped — no casualties. Bombs were dropped to west in the camp.	
		1.15	The small wooden latrines were not quite possibly drawn away	
		2.30	Argn Comd visited Base Cmdant & he was about in Surgical Treatment Depot by Boat	
			No officers	
		4.15	Enemy aircraft appeared not enough to bother us in camp. They were engaged on our aircraft and by our aircraft guns and had disappeared by 4.30 a.m.	
			Leaving Town were reported On Motor car to leave FONTINETTE Station	
			CALAIS at 2.30 with the train, troop 5 from 12.15/- leaving at 12.45/-	
			Reinforcements to and the same clearly of 13 — for STAPLES	
		9.30	England began to suspect Belgonne camp, & fast no transport. A lot enemy	
			through the tragic	
		10.20	Still light to come to GRAVELINES & Camp & replaces officers. They were	
	10.5.18		armed and strong, had took extra	
		2.15	Signal Shelters was constructed of 15m ft 2	
		4—	Privates Popular and assisted the FONTINETTE Station	

WAR DIARY
or
INTELLIGENCE SUMMARY.
(Erase heading not required.)

Army Form C. 2118.

Place	Date	Hour	Summary of Events and Information	Remarks and references to Appendices
CALAIS	10.5.18	1.25 pm	Arrived at Station and entrained as ordered.	
		4.10 pm	Finished entraining on arrival in train also a train officer on duty any enemy	57/1
		4.25 pm	Train started. 34 tumbrils (C waggons (Hors) 24 stalls. 1 van left behind	
ST OMER		4 am	Train stopped. Self + horse for an hour. Left with 30th	
BRIAS		10 am	arrived at the xxxx and entrained (part ?) x xxxx xxx Received	
			59th Division to remain at BRIAS Station instead of marching to SAIN LES PERNES Made necessary sanitary arrangements for use of men. Parkes transport Menmdept under horsed and in artill yard.	
BRIAS	11.5.18	5 am	Breakfast. March off en route for VIELFORT at 8 am.	
VIELFORT	11.5.18	Noon	Arrived.	
		12.10 pm	Colonel, medical officer + adjutant visit camp on hill; Tents (75) allotted to officers + companies (3 cupts 4 subs 16 ad 17 men per tent).	
		12.35 pm	(Colonel + visited me of Major gen. ROMER, in gen 59th Div. He asks who we were, when the Colonel reports + said no FATHER, gen. Romer and we were his children, + he would be like Father + Grandfather	57/1
	12.5.18	12.30 pm	Saw ahead + pick from R.E. of DIVION for Track work	R.2/5
		5 pm	2/Lt Exler missing when ambulance arrived to take him to Hospital.	

Army Form C. 2118.

WAR DIARY
or
INTELLIGENCE SUMMARY.
(Erase heading not required.)

Instructions regarding War Diaries and Intelligence Summaries are contained in F. S. Regs., Part II and the Staff Manual respectively. Title pages will be prepared in manuscript.

Place	Date	Hour	Summary of Events and Information	Remarks and references to Appendices
VIELFORT	13.5.16	8.30 a.m	Battalion left camp for fighting trenches	
			Hear that 2/Lt Eales has reported himself at some hospital at Bray. Report sent to Brigade re this officer	
VIELFORT	14.5.16	6.30 a.m	Battalion goes to work	
	15.5.16	"	Battalion goes to work	
	16 "	"	"	
	17 "	"	"	
	18 "	"	"	
	19 "	"	"	
	20 "	"	Reveille at 3.30 a.m. Battalion goes to work, 5 a.m. SD training, 5-6 p.m.	
	21 "	"	"	
	22 "	"	"	
	23 "	"	"	
	24 "	"	"	
	25 "	"	"	
	26 "	9 a.m	Battalion goes on parade for training. Major Gen Bennis short inspects Bn at training	
	27 "		Reveille at 3.30 a.m. B Coy goes to work 5 a.m. Bn training 5-6 p.m. remainder of day	
	28 "		Reveille 4.30 a.m. B and D work 5 a.m. Bn training 5-6 p.m. rest of day	BRAY again shelled
	29 "			BRAY again shelled. 1 a.m. shell at night
	30 "			BRAY - HOUDAIN shelled, shells near 12 noon

Army Form C. 2118.

WAR DIARY
or
INTELLIGENCE SUMMARY.

(Erase heading not required.)

Instructions regarding War Diaries and Intelligence Summaries are contained in F. S. Regs., Part II. and the Staff Manual respectively. Title pages will be prepared in manuscript.

Place	Date	Hour	Summary of Events and Information	Remarks and references to Appendices
VIELFORT WOOD.	31.5.18.	10.30 p.m.	Work on yesterday. BRUAY & HOUDAIN shelled. Civil population began to leave HOUDAIN. Air raid at night.	

Hugo K.S. Woodhouse
Colonel
Commanding 11th Battalion Somerset L.I. (T.F.)

(CONFIDENTIAL)

11TH (G.S.) BATTALION SOMERSET LIGHT INFANTRY

Army Form C. 2118.

WAR DIARY
or
INTELLIGENCE SUMMARY
JUNE 1918

(Erase heading not required.)

Instructions regarding War Diaries and Intelligence Summaries are contained in F. S. Regs., Part II. and the Staff Manual respectively. Title pages will be prepared in manuscript.

Place	Date	Hour	Summary of Events and Information	Remarks and references to Appendices
VIELFORT WOOD	1-6-18	6 a.m.	Battalion paraded for work. BRUAY & HOUDAIN shelled.	
		11 a.m.	Two 15-inch shells burst near working party. One man slightly wounded on night fatigue by shell fragment. NAME: 17971 Pte. Clark F. "C" Coy. This was the Battalion first casualty.	
"	2-6-18	9 p.m.	Air Raid at night.	
"	3-6-18	6 a.m.	Battalion did training till 1 p.m. Air raid at night. BRUAY & HOUDAIN shelled.	
"	4-6-18	6 a.m.	Battalion paraded for work. BRUAY & HOUDAIN shelled. Air raid at night; bombs dropped in neighbouring camp	
"	5-6-18	6 a.m.	Note – 1st August Course received from Brigade. Draft of 11 men received from Base.	
"	6-6-18	6 a.m.	Received from Brigade letter showing 5 men aux per Brigade. Note from Brigade reinforced drawn 2 NCO's & 10 men per Battalion. Wire received later to the day relieving 4 men reinforcements to the Battalion.	
			Stating note of 4-6-18 stand read "5 men aux per Battn."	
"	7.6.18	6 a.m.	Battalion paraded for work.	
		2.30 p.m.	Inspection of Transport by Divisional Inspector of Transport. Very satisfactory.	
		2.30 p.m.	Sport at "At Home" of R.F.A. Brigade (84th) in camped in the Valley. C.O., Adjutant & several other Officers attended.	
		6.30 p.m.	G.O.C. Xth Corps, Lieut. General Sir W.E. PEYTON, K.C.B. K.C.V.O. D.S.O. inspected the Battalion at training. No special remarks.	

WAR DIARY
or
INTELLIGENCE SUMMARY.
(Erase heading not required.)

Army Form C. 2118.

Place	Date	Hour	Summary of Events and Information	Remarks and references to Appendices
VIELFORT WOOD	8.6.18	6 am	Battalion paraded for work.	
"	"	11 am	Capt. W.E.L. FOWLER, R.A.M.C., was taken to Field Ambulance at ESTRÉE CAUCHIE, and is general and various men in hot weather, subsequently admitted to 42nd C.C.S., RUBIGNY.	1/F
"	"	3 pm	Lt. J.I. MOSLEY went to ESTRÉE CAUCHIE, & selected 2,100 francs for pay from Field Cashier X Corps. The Battalion received enemy fire.	
"	9-6-18	2.15 am	Reveille. Companies handed off independently & took up their position in B.B. line	
"	"	5.30 am	Battalion H.Q. & signallers left camp.	
OLHAIN WOOD	"	8 am	Reports received at Battalion H.Q. states all companies in position - Kinston	2/F
"	"	11 am	The acting Divisional Commander, Brig. Gen. C.H.L. JAMES, C.B., C.M.G., visited Battalion H.Q. & said he was satisfied with the Battalion performance. Companies marched back to camp.	
VIELFORT WOOD	10.6.18	8 am	Battalion paraded for work.	
"	"	5 pm	Capt. F.C. SMITH, M.O.R.C., U.S.A. reported for duty during the temporary absence of Capt	2/F
"	"	6.30 pm	W.E.L. FOWLER. 2/Lieut D.T. MORGAN was sent to 2/3 N.M. Field Ambulance at ESTRÉE CAUCHIE with a weak.	
"	11.6.18	6 am	Battalion paraded for work, Project outman new for transport to La Thiloire, Aubigny, are called by some.	
"	"	11 am	Col. DENNIS, R.A.M.C., inspected 25th men who had been reported as unfit by the Battn M.O.	2/F
"	"	"	Recut: - B1, 200, - 13.2 - 42 - 13.3 - 12	
"	"	2.30pm	2/Lieut V.LIEUT VIELFORT WOOD for CHABLI 4 NEUF in advance flow with transport. 71.s84-"B-" R.F.A. left. 2/Lt. L.V. HARDY & 5 men of 72 73 D.L. & 2 men of the 13th (S) R West Riding Regiment were temporary attached to the Battalion.	3/F

WAR DIARY
INTELLIGENCE SUMMARY

Army Form C. 2118.

Place	Date	Hour	Summary of Events and Information	Remarks and references to Appendices
VIELFORT (Wood)	12-6-18	6 am	Battalion paraded for work	
"	13-6-18	6 am	Battalion paraded for work	
"	14-6-18	6 am	Battalion paraded for work	
"	"	11 pm	Wire from 177 Brigade, ordering no work on G.Q. line to last day which was to be a day of rest.	
"	"	11.45 pm	Wire from 177 Brigade to cancel above order, and return work considered B.B. line next day.	
"	15-6-18	6 am	Battalion paraded for work	
"	"	10 am	All available Officers met the C.O. at B.B. Line & did a tactical scheme	
"	"	6 pm	Orders from Brigade received to prepare to move the next day. A circular from Division detailing stores and war kit to be put the Brigade kingt two months rations, to held guard party cadre of above	
"	16-6-18	4.30 pm	message received from 177 Brigade, marching Battalion to move at 6-0 pm to AUCHEL	
"	"	6.20 pm	Battalion marched off via DIVION and CALONNE RICOUART. Baggage party left later 3/p. A.O. M.and	
AUCHEL	"	8-45 am	Battalion arrived at AUCHEL, & took over billets from 11th Royal Scots Fusiliers 1 Company occupied Ste remainder of the Battalion were in billets in the mining officers & private houses Hy Qrs at a Estaminet	
"	"	shop Forty. There had been fallen into its march		
"	"	11 am	Field cooker arrived by a different route	
"	"	12 noon	Breakfast	
"	"	6 pm	Capt Milloy returned from M.T.(UMBER)	
"	"	11.45 pm	Last load of Baggage arrived. Brigade had only sent one lorry, which did not report at VIELFORT until 4-30 pm. It subsequently they made 2 journeys to & fro.	
"	"	11.30 pm	Hostile aircraft dropped bombs, one 50 yds of the Mens Billets Orders received from Brigade to receive march to SAINS- LEZ- PERNES, next day at 5-45 a.m.	

Army Form C. 2118.

WAR DIARY
or
INTELLIGENCE SUMMARY.
(Erase heading not required.)

Instructions regarding War Diaries and Intelligence Summaries are contained in F.S. Regs., Part II. and the Staff Manual respectively. Title pages will be prepared in manuscript.

Place	Date	Hour	Summary of Events and Information	Remarks and references to Appendices
AUCHEL	17-6-18	5 am	Reveille Battalion marched off. Leaving half of party under 2/Lt H.O. Ward & 2/Lt W.L. Brown (sick) nor. fit to come on with baggage party. Capt. R.N. Ridler & two cyclists went ahead to billeting party.	
"	"	6 am	Heavy rain for two miles and CAUCHY-A-LA-TOUR, FLORINGHEM & PERNES the Battalion arrived at SHINS-LEZ-PERNES. Billeting was difficult - ? by an in-ln-lb the commanders learned return and Officers found ind, and one man in huts & some in entrance. Newspapers particular in a cottage near centre of village. One hundred & ninety-two men had fallen out in its march & the new party, seventy, procured lorries from the Canadian at AUCHEL.	21A
SHINS-LEZ-PERNES	"	10-15am		
"	"	11.45pm	2/Lt H.O. Ward arrived with its new party.	27A
"	18-6-18	9 am	Transport Officer reported one man & a quantity of detained effects of AUCHEL. Col. C. Friends was traced attached to ENGLAND at about 8.30am. & H.Q.C. & BRANTHAM.	
"	"	9.30 am	C.O. went to Brigade Hence. to Dinner at BONY, when to mix with Divisional Commander Maj. Gen. Sir R.D. WHIGHAM K.C.B., D.S.O. & one officer from the 59th Division was to be the prisoner.	
"	"	5pm	B.1. Dinner, for keeping good acts of Battalion. C.O. Ld Officers meeting, it discussed what to had hand of Division & its own expansion. Infantry Battalion Training to begin at once. Capt. W.E.L. Foster, R.A.M.C. returned from C.C.S.	31A
"	19-6-18		Battalion trained according to program of work submitted to Brigade. Capt. F.C. Smith, M.O.R.C. U.S.A. attd to rejoin #2 N.M. Field Ambulance	32A
"	20-6-18		Battalion trained according to program of work. Brig. Gen. C.H.L. James visited Battalion at training.	
"	21-6-15	6pm	C.O., 2nd in command, & Adjutant attended meeting at Brigade H.Qs at HESTRUS. Orders received to be ready to move to new area. Saturday or Sunday	33A

Army Form C. 2118.

WAR DIARY
or
INTELLIGENCE SUMMARY.
(Erase heading not required.)

Place	Date	Hour	Summary of Events and Information	Remarks and references to Appendices
SAINS-LEZ-PERNES	22/6/18	8am	Battalion sent 110 men per hour to halt at PERNES. These men had to march to Anzin-lez-	
		6	make to procure with transport.	
		1pm	Orders received to move to DELETTE on Monday June 24th.	
		10.am	Battalion rested.	
"	23/6/18	11am	A + B Companies started to march towards DELETTE to march past Maj. Gen. Whigham palate staff	
"	24/6/18	3pm	C + D Companies followed in turn. Heavy rain commenced	
"		3.40pm	A & B headed the column & C & D took up the march.	
"		7.30pm	C & D Companies arrived at DELETTE owing to it's passage of a squadron of Canadian Light Horse heavily was difficult, but all its Battalion was finally sorted for the night. The G.O.C. Division watched C & D Companies march into the Town, & Brig. Gen. Jarvis watched after march	
LAIRES DELETTE			past Battalion H.Q. Battalion continued Training. Two hundred & 80 other Ranks at PONEHE	
"	25.6.18 26-6.18	9-4.5am 10-7-30 5-11pm	Start march in two motors Capt Q.W.N FRASER went off Sent to ? with Limberge Reinft Set.? factory	
"	27/6/18	7am	Fifty B" & B"" other Ranks was sent at Labour Corps Base Depot at BOULOGNE	
		8.45 am	Battalion continued Training	
		10am	Orders received from Brigade to be prepared to move within 12 hours This was later extended to 9 am the next day	

WAR DIARY
or
INTELLIGENCE SUMMARY
(Erase heading not required.)

Army Form C. 2118.

Place	Date	Hour	Summary of Events and Information	Remarks and references to Appendices
DELETTE	18.6.18	8 am	Battalion paraded for final action. Divisional orders	
		8.10	H.Q. & Baggage party with 15 LEWIS moved to AUDINGHUN via OVERCOQUES, & VENNEGROENEN Capt R.H. CLARK.	
			B I coy for empty rail dep as below if poss.	
AUDINGHUN	19.6.18	4 pm	Battalion arrived. Headquarters put up with farm near 1st Church	
		8.15 am	Battalion entered training. Lieut. C. Marles went to a Divisional Signal Course RUDISAY.	
		2.6 pm	(Transport Inspection (Divisional) W.O.R.	
		4 pm	Lieut J.I. Morley returned from instructing duty.	
	20.6.18	9-15 am	Battalion went to camp near VINELY. Route marched. Forty eight road closely wanted inspected	
		8-40pm	2/Lieut TOSLAND of the H.T.M.G. to demonstrate Button refused & reorganized in Coy.	

Rupert S. Woolhouse
Lt Col
Commanding 11th (Service) Batt (General Service 17?)

2.7.18

Confidential

Army Form C. 2118.

WAR DIARY
11th Bn Somerset Light Infantry
INTELLIGENCE SUMMARY

July 1918

Place	Date	Hour	Summary of Events and Information	Remarks and references to Appendices
AUDINCTHUN	1.7.18	8.45 am	Battalion paraded for Training. Major F.A.W. How brevetted over as F.G.C.M. at H.Q. 25th K.R.R.C.	
		5 P.M.	Evening parade cancelled by Brigade as the Battalion had worked hard at musketry the day before	
"	2.7.18	8.45 am	Battalion paraded for training. The Commanding Officer read out a letter of greeting to the Consolidated division (59) now about to take its place in the British line, from Field Marshal Sir Douglas Haig. This letter stated that he fully recognised the arduous physical limitations, and that they would not be given tasks beyond their powers.	
		12.30 P.M.	A telephone message came from Brigade stating that two German aeroplanes had been brought down during the night, and that one man of their crews was still at large, the battalion was to be sent out at once to search the locality when he was believed to be.	
		1.20 P.M.	Brigade Telephoned to say that men must have been dim now before starting the search. Two could not be done, as they had already started out.	
		6-7 P.M.	The Companies returned Tired & hungry, however sad and no trail since 7.30 AM search unsuccessful.	
"	3.7.18	8.45 am 5 PM	Telegram received that the missing man was found Training as usual	

Confidential

WAR DIARY
or
INTELLIGENCE SUMMARY

1 Bn Somerset Light Infantry

Army Form C. 2118.

(Erase heading not required.)

Instructions regarding War Diaries and Intelligence Summaries are contained in F.S. Regs., Part II. and the Staff Manual respectively. Title pages will be prepared in manuscript.

Place	Date	Hour	Summary of Events and Information	Remarks and references to Appendices
AUDINCTHUN	4/7/18	8.45 am	Training as usual	
		1 PM	The Divisional General Service Officers joined the Battalion from the Base. Lt TELEMACHE, 2/Lt SHAW, 2/Lt SKILLING, 2/Lt DUGAN, 2/Lt WITHY, 2/Lt LE BRUN, 2/Lt COLEGATE.	5/5
	5.7.18	8.45 am	Training as usual	
		5 PM	Battalion paraded for whist scheme. A and B Coys relieving C & D. Relief complete was reported at 12.30 PM. The Cookers were in attendance & tea was provided at 6 PM.	5/5
	6.7.18	12.30 am	Returned to Billets & turn in. The Div'nal and Bde Commanders were in attendance with staff.	
		9.30 am	Breakfasts.	
		5-6.30 PM	Recreational Training.	
	7.7.18	8.45 am, 5 PM	Battalion parades as usual	
	8.7.18	8 am	Received notice 4 hrs before to move	5/5
		8.45 am	Parade for Training	
		2 PM	All Officers available + 2 NCOs per Coy. Attended to witness Trench mortar demonstration attack by Demonstration Platoon H.A.C. Most instructive. Div'l & Bde Cmdrs were present	

Confidential

Army Form C. 2118.

1/1 Batt'n Somerset L.I.

WAR DIARY
or
INTELLIGENCE SUMMARY.
(Erase heading not required.)

Instructions regarding War Diaries and Intelligence Summaries are contained in F. S. Regs., Part II. and the Staff Manual respectively. Title pages will be prepared in manuscript.

Place	Date	Hour	Summary of Events and Information	Remarks and references to Appendices
AUDINGHEN	8.7.18	4.30 pm	Lt Brooks + men from School of Signals returned. He went for instruction but was put on to instruct 3H Instructors.	5/A
		5 pm	Battalion paraded for Training.	
		6 pm	Telegram from Brigade with Instructions about move.	
	9.7.18	8 am	Route march cancelled by brigade and next days programme instituted.	
		8.45 am	Battalion parade as ordered.	
			Capt R. Ben. went T/R to West Staps. Left at RUISSEAUVILLE for Billets	
		11 pm	Move Orders arrived from Brigade	
	10.7.18	4 am	Reveille	7/B
		5 am	Breakfast	
		6 am	C&D Coys paraded at Church under Major How marched to MONTGOVILLE, thence by bus not by A and B Coys via LONDES, who entrained C&D Coys proceeded by bus, and A and B marched, Transport proceeded separately. Arrived C+	
			D Coys at MONTEVILLE	
		12.30 pm	Arrival at billets	
		1 pm	Dinners.	
RUISSEAUVILLE			The rest of the day was spent in settling into billets & finding Parade Grounds. A short visit was paid by the Divisional General during the evening.	7/B

Confidential

Army Form C. 2118.

WAR DIARY
or
INTELLIGENCE SUMMARY.
(Erase heading not required.)

1st Bn Somerset L.I.

Instructions regarding War Diaries and Intelligence Summaries are contained in F.S. Regs., Part II. and the Staff Manual respectively. Title pages will be prepared in manuscript.

Place	Date	Hour	Summary of Events and Information	Remarks and references to Appendices
RUISSEAUVILLE	11.7.18	8.45 am	During the morning Companies were out reconnoitring for Coy Billets and training ground and carried on the usual training. A Mat was prepared by the Brigade Commander for instruction of Bn.	5/B
		3 pm	A detachment of 1 Officer and 16 O.R's of RE were attached to us for billets & Rations.	
"	12.7.18	8.45 am	Parade as usual. Lieut Brookes left for base to be Medically Boarded. 2/Lt M. Fox then Battalion Signals Lt Johnstone went to Hospital.	5/B
		11 am	Capt Bulteel attended Attack Conference at Brigade H.Q.	
"	13.7.18	8.45 am	Training as usual	
		2.30 pm	Visit by Army Commander. Coy & Platoon Drill, Gas, PT and 9 A/Platoons were carried out	
"	14.7.18	9.30 am	Church Parade. 2/Lt Ross left for XIII Corps Lewis Gun School.	
"	15.7.18	8.45 am	Training as usual	
		5.30 pm	Lecture by Batt. Commander to all officers at the Cinema house CANLERS on Trench Warfare. A Terrific thunderstorm prevailed all night & rain about 6 am. Summer lightning was extremely vivid.	7/B

Confidential (1/13th Somerset L.I.)

WAR DIARY or INTELLIGENCE SUMMARY.

(Erase heading not required.)

Army Form C. 2118.

Place	Date	Hour	Summary of Events and Information	Remarks and references to Appendices
RUISSEAUVILLE	16/7/18	8.15 am	160 Old men and Officers were sent before the Medical Board at H.Q. 2/2nd Bn. to meet Lt.Col. by ADMS. Capt Sherwood and Capt Allen were both marked downs which would mean Vacancies among Coy Commanders.	3)/5
			Brigade was taken over by Lt Col Woodhouse DSO, the Bde Commander having gone home on leave. Col Woodhouse went over took up Quarters at Brigade HQ. The Command of the Battalion was taken over by Major Horn.	
	17.7.18	8.45 am	Training was carried out as per weekly programme, and Battalion was inspected in Drill Order by Major Horn.	3)/5
		5.PM	Parade as usual.	
		10.30 PM to 11PM	Short march around country in war kit/outfit. Scouts out a small scheme.	
	18.7.18	8.45 am	Training as usual. Battalion Band Franks send on Tunica.	
	19.7.18		Orders arrived that the Companies went to proceed up the line on the 21st to be attached to 11th Division for Instruction. B and C Coys were chosen & steps were taken to ensure that they were properly fitted up. Helmets were painted & covered to put in battle + foot out was carried out in their places in training from out Brigade. Marching program of Training was strictly adhered to training was not hindered.	
	20.7.18		Many contradictory orders with regard to move. Final orders arrived at 10PM and were immediately circulated to Companies without	3)/5

D.D. & L., London, E.C.
(A10266) Wt W5300/P713 750,000 2/18 Sch. S2 Forms/C2118/16

Army Form C. 2118.

WAR DIARY
or
INTELLIGENCE SUMMARY.   11 Bn Somerset LI.

(Erase heading not required.)

Place	Date	Hour	Summary of Events and Information	Remarks and references to Appendices
ROSSEAUVILLE	21.7.18	9pm 1pm	Church Parade. Two Companies B and C under the command of Major Hoyt together with the Adjutant Capt. Bulden and Acting Quartermaster Lt. Campbell proceeded by bus to Camp SIDING. 6th Londons who were in the front line with the 33rd Bn 11th Bmn at RUTOIRE ALLEY. In readiness they were first to return, the Companies having been assembled, and they had to retrace their steps to the HQ of 33rd I Bde at (CHATEAU MAZINGARE) these arrived tired + hungry	2/5
	22.7.18	3am	after having for 8 miles. Major Hoyt was billeted in the Chateau. The Adjutant + Lt Campbell in the floor of a deserted Estaminet kindly provided by the Town Major. Next morning the 2 Bn Ldns Coys + the 2 Coys were suitably embarked + sent back to the 33rd Bde + given instructions to proceed to FRAMECOURT instead of FRAMECOURT which was a ※ Clerical error instead of FR on the part of Either the 11th or 59th Divn	3/5
		5.15pm	The two Companies entrained and proceeded to Thursday CAVEUX, but on arrival they were instructed by the 59 Divn to proceed to FRAMECOURT from where they started.	
		9.25 AM	They reached Fillets.	
		8.45AM	The other two Companies went for a route march via TRAMECOURT, AMBRICOURT + CANLERS under command of Capt. Hopkins.	

Confidential

Army Form C. 2118.

WAR DIARY
or
INTELLIGENCE SUMMARY.   11.Bh Somerset L.I.

(Erase heading not required.)

Instructions regarding War Diaries and Intelligence Summaries are contained in F. S. Regs., Part II. and the Staff Manual respectively. Title pages will be prepared in manuscript.

Place	Date	Hour	Summary of Events and Information	Remarks and references to Appendices
Russeauville	23.7.18	8:45 am	Battalion Training as usual.	
"	24.7.18	8.30 am	Orders arrive to move, but no definite instructions were given. The Battalion carried on its training as usual.	51h
		11 P.M.	Still no definite orders.	
"	25.7.18	2.30 am	Orders arrived twice immediately issued.	
		6.22 AM.	Transport left Billets.	
		8 AM.	Two lorries came and collected Baggage.	
		12.30 am	Battalion paraded and marched to CAMBLERS & made there they entrained & were taken by train to BELLACOURT.	59h
		9.30 pm	Arrival & settle into Billets.	
BELLACOURT	26.7.18	8.45	Battalion inspected by Major How in drill order. Settle into billets. Inlying Piquet grounds &c.	
		11.15	Coys clean up billets. Rifles cleaned & inspected.	59h

Confidential

Army Form C. 2118.

Instructions regarding War Diaries and Intelligence
Summaries are contained in F. S. Regs., Part II.
and the Staff Manual respectively. Title pages
will be prepared in manuscript.

WAR DIARY
or
INTELLIGENCE SUMMARY.
1138. 1st Lincolns.
(Erase heading not required.)

Place	Date	Hour	Summary of Events and Information	Remarks and references to Appendices
BELLACOURT	27.7.18	8.45 am	Coy Platoon Training. 2 Lts COLEGATE and MANNERS Visited the Front Line.	2/1/5
		5 pm	Recreational Training.	
"	28.7.18	9.30 am	Battalion paraded for divine service.	3/1/5
			Voluntary service Holy Communion followed by Open air service.	
		7 pm	Lts STRATFORD, SHAND and TOLLEMACHE visited the Line.	
	29.7.18	8.45 am to 5 pm	Battalion headed for Training	7/1/5
			2/Lts PILCHER and AITKEN visited the Trenches	
			Capt RIDLEY, 2/Lt DRAPER, Lt MOSLEY and Lt NEWNHAM toured the artillery for instruction in co-operation.	
	29.7.18		Training for Musketry	
		5.30	Lecture by Bde Major on Machine gun. Lt Col WOOLHOUSE D.S.O. was present.	
		8 pm	Battalion had practice march to assembly position near BLAIREVILLE	5/1/5
		10.30 pm	March After reporting arrival they returned to billets	

Confidential

Army Form C. 2118.

WAR DIARY
or
INTELLIGENCE SUMMARY. 11 Bn Somerset L.I.

(Erase heading not required.)

Instructions regarding War Diaries and Intelligence Summaries are contained in F. S. Regs., Part II. and the Staff Manual respectively. Title pages will be prepared in manuscript.

Place	Date	Hour	Summary of Events and Information	Remarks and references to Appendices
BELLACOURT	30/7/18	9.45 am	Training was carried out as usual	
		5.30 AM	"A" line on Co-Operation of Artillery with Infantry at the Village school GROSVILLE. Lt Col W.H.K.S Woodhouse relinquished Command of Brigade, the Brigade Commander having returned from leave & took over Command of the Battalion.	
	31/7/18	8.45 am	Training was as usual.	
		5 PM	Parade for training.	
		5.45 PM	Four Shrapnel shells burst in the Village, wounding L/Cpl Sommers W.G. L.Cpl Locke E.H. and Pte Fogg (Slight) Also wounding a small child about 10 years of age. First aid was promptly rendered by the M.O.	

Hugo W.S. Worthington
Lt-Col

"CONFIDENTIAL"

Army Form C. 2118.

5.P.
5 sheets

~ AUGUST 1918 ~
11th Batt. Somerset Light Infantry

WAR DIARY
or
INTELLIGENCE SUMMARY.
(Erase heading not required.)

Instructions regarding War Diaries and Intelligence Summaries are contained in F. S. Regs., Part II. and the Staff Manual respectively. Title pages will be prepared in manuscript.

Vol 4

Place	Date	Hour	Summary of Events and Information	Remarks and references to Appendices
BELLACOURT	2.8.18	9 a.m.	Instruction by Coy. Commanders prior to moving off to the trenches.	
"	"	8 p.m.	Marched to CHAT MAIGRE Strong Point. Sht. 51cSW M19. Meeting guides at 9.30 p.m. at the trenches in WAILLY Sht. 51cSE Pts. 90 & 80. There was no hostile shelling during the relief which was completed at 1.15 a.m.	65
"	3.8.18	1.15 a.m.		65
TRENCHES	3.8.18	5 p.m.	Most of the day was spent in improving trenches, drawing kit, and rebuilding dug-outs. Inspection of rifles and gas respirators carried out.	65
"	4.8.18	10 p.m.	Hostile shelling on our sector plunging rather desultory, and our casualties were: 1 man killed, 1 man wounded also 1 minor wounds. Mules were killed, the wounded sent back. M.K.S. and one was wounded but it's poor that hosts be shot.	65
"	6.8.18	10 a.m.	Our Aircraft were very heavily shelled between 10 a.m. & 12 noon and 5 p.m. & 7 p.m. Three aeroplanes to be on board.	65
"	"	11.45 a.m.	Two [observation?] balloons flown over our lines towards the Boches, but they appeared to be shot down by L.G. fire before getting well into the Boche line.	65
"	"	4 p.m.	Another [large observation?] balloon broke from its moorings and went well over the Boche line and disappeared out of sight.	65
"	"	8.15	The Battalion Scouts to move up to the Front line. Owing to rain the trenches were in a very bad state which made the work extremely difficult.	65
"	6.8.18	10 a.m.	The Enemy blanks to to shell R.H.Q. but were not successful in obtaining a hit of any kind.	65
"	7.8.18	all day	This day was passed very quietly. Nothing of interest occurred.	65
"	8.8.18	"	Specialist Officers came up to have a look around prior to taking over the area.	65
"	"	9 p.m.	Relief of Battalion by M.A.R.E.I. Arch M. for BAPRY. The relief was completed in subsequently quiet and continued through at 12.30 p.m.	65
"	9.8.18	9 a.m.	Arrival of our destination and marched to BARLY. That breakfast and remainder of day was spent in resting.	65

(A10266) Wt. W4390/1773 750,000 9/16 Sch. 92 Forms/C2118/16   D. D. & L., London, E.C.

Army Form C. 2118.

WAR DIARY
or
INTELLIGENCE SUMMARY.
(Erase heading not required.)

Instructions regarding War Diaries and Intelligence Summaries are contained in F. S. Regs., Part II. and the Staff Manual respectively. Title pages will be prepared in manuscript.

Place	Date	Hour	Summary of Events and Information	Remarks and references to Appendices
BARLY	10.8.18	9 a.m.	The Battalion was inspected by the C.O. and afterwards the Companies went on with their training.	
"	11.8.18	10.30 a.m.	Church Parade on the Brigade Parade ground. Remainder of day was given over to resting.	
"	12.8.18	9 a.m.	The Battalion continues training under Company arrangements.	
"	13.8.18	"	"	
"	14.8.18	"	"	
"	15.8.18	2/-	The Battalion were inspected by the Corps Commander who expressed himself highly pleased with the turn-out on parade.	
"	16.8.18	7 a.m.	The Battalion marches off to BELACOURT arriving about 6 p.m.	
BELACOURT	17.8.18	all day	This day was spent in cleaning up billets &c.	
"	18.8.18	9 a.m.	The C.O. inspects the Battalion on the Parade ground, and afterwards training was proceeded with.	
"	19.8.18	9 a.m.	Training was continues under Company arrangements.	
"	20.8.18	11.30 a.m.	The Battalion marches off to the PURPLE LINE trenches 51 S.E. A R 26. 36. Taking up their position in good time.	
TRENCHES	21.8.18	all day	Quinchy new alise. Surrounding villages were bombed by the Boches during the night. One bomb unfortunately fell on one of A Co's billets killing 2 men and wounding 2 men.	
"	"	"	Enemy aircraft made three attempts to get through, but only one succeeds in getting through. Our aircraft brought down our lines on bombing raids. One appeared to be downed by our Lewis and Hotchkiss fire in WALLY area.	
"	23.8.18		Left the trenches and marches off to SAULTY arriving about 11 a.m. Bivouacs for the night.	
SAULTY	24.8.18	10 a.m.	Marches from SAULTY along railway to L'ARBRET then entraining and leaving at 2 p.m. arrives at BAQUETTE station about 8.15 p.m. then marches to MAZINGHAM.	
MAZINGHAM	25.8.18	all day	This day was spent in resting and cleaning up.	

Army Form C. 2118.

WAR DIARY
or
INTELLIGENCE SUMMARY.
(Erase heading not required.)

Instructions regarding War Diaries and Intelligence Summaries are contained in F. S. Regs. Part II. and the Staff Manual respectively. Title pages will be prepared in manuscript.

Place	Date	Hour	Summary of Events and Information	Remarks and references to Appendices
MALINGHAM	26.8.18	2/2	The Battalion left for ROBECQUÉ travelling by motor lorry and arriving about 4 p.m. went into reserve, relieving the R.W.F.	90
ROBECQUÉ	27.8.18	1.15	After a quiet day the Battalion marched off for Front Line, then relieving the 12th Batt. S.W.I. The relief was carried out satisfactorily.	90
TRENCHES	28.8.18	All day	Front line companies reported numerous fire starts by the enemy, and it was found he was retreating quickly. The only serious opposition offered to our advance was M.G. Fire. The sky at night was lit up by the many fires started by the enemy	90
"	29.8.18	"	Enemy still retiring, and LESTREM was observed to be on fire at various places. We continued to keep in touch with the enemy who went back rapidly.	90
"	30.8.18	"	Enemy fire still prominent and enemy still retiring. The Battalion received orders to go forward to EPINETTE. Advanced there and established headquarters.	90
EPINETTE	31.8.18	"	Spent the day here and received orders to hold ourselves in readiness to relieve the 15th Batt. Essex Reg. who were in front line just through LESTREM.	90

J. W. Hoys
Capt.
15 L.I

CONFIDENTIAL

Army Form C. 2118.

SEPTEMBER 1918
11th Batt. Somerset Light Infantry
WAR DIARY
or
INTELLIGENCE SUMMARY.
(Erase heading not required.)

Instructions regarding War Diaries and Intelligence Summaries are contained in F. S. Regs., Part II. and the Staff Manual respectively. Title pages will be prepared in manuscript.

Place	Date	Hour	Summary of Events and Information	Remarks and references to Appendices
EPINETTE	1.9.18	6 a.m.	The Batt. marches from EPINETTE to LESTREM thus relieving the 16th Batt. Essex Regt. Heavy shelling and the Batt. arriving in LESTREM. Our front line troops were soon in touch with the enemy and spotted them still retreating.	LESTREM GD 36SE2
TRENCHES	2.9.18	all day	After a quiet night the enemy shelled various parts of LESTREM but not very heavily. Our front line troops advanced, but were met with much M.G. fire. During the night the enemy again shelled LESTREM at intervals. There were still being shots in the enemy and the continuous shell about. We were relieved by the 9th D of W R during the evening and the Batt. then marched to a spot just outside MERVILLE line, bivouacking for the night.	GD
ST. VENANT	3.9.18	1.30 p.m.	The Batt. marched off by road for ST. VENANT reaching LILLE ROAD about 6.30 p.m. being billets in the Anglais.	GD
"	4.9.18	all day	This day was spent in bathing and general cleaning up. Orders were received to Lancers again to EPINETTE	GD
"	5.9.18	11 a.m.	The Batt. continued for LACONNÉ and marched from there by road to EPINETTE. G & H Coys heavy parties and bivouacs for the night	GD
EPINETTE	6.9.18	all day	Cleaning up equipment and rifles for inspection. Messages received stating the Batt. would relieve LLP in the Sector in the morning. No enemy order came through this day	GD
"	7.9.18	2 p.m.	The Batt. moves off by road to PONT RIQUEL just EAST of LESTREM, arriving about 4 p.m. It was shelled by the enemy between 9.30 p.m. & 10.30 p.m.	GD
PONT RIQUEL	8.9.18	all day	Hostile shelling during the early hours of the morning.	GD
"	9.9.18	"	Hostile shelling during the night. The weather broke & changed for the worst, and subsequent rain made conditions not so cheerful.	GD
"	10.9.18	"	The weather continued bad and the rain came down heavily. Hostile shelling by the enemy during the night and road tracks of the sector.	GD
"	11.9.18	7.15 —	Gas bombs & inspection. Weather better but changeable afternoon	GD
"	12.9.18	Early hours	Early bombs & inspection. Fatigues and repair work on roads and dug-outs under bombs	GD

D.D. & L., London, E.C. (A10266) W.t W5300/P713 750,000 2/18 Sch. 53 Forms/C2118/16

CONFIDENTIAL

Army Form C. 2118.

September 1918
11th Batt. Somerset Light Infantry

WAR DIARY
or
INTELLIGENCE SUMMARY.
(Erase heading not required.)

Instructions regarding War Diaries and Intelligence Summaries are contained in F. S. Regs., Part II. and the Staff Manual respectively. Title pages will be prepared in manuscript.

Place	Date	Hour	Summary of Events and Information	Remarks and references to Appendices
PONT RIQUEUL	13.9.18	All day	Orders were received for the Batt. to proceed to the Front line N.E. of Gravenelle. The Batt fell in on the R.W.F. Parade ground and moved off at 4.30 p.m. Tea was served out at MUDDY LANE. Proceeding the Batt arrived at about 8 p.m. and the relief was carried out successfully.	AU6 & RS 36 S.W.1. GD
TRENCHES	14.9.18	"	Hostile shelling over B.H.Q. during the early hours of the morning. Enemy artillery active between 11 a.m & 1 p.m. on the whole of our front during the day. Lively & continuous shelling round B.H.Q. by the enemy from about 10 p.m - 12.1 a.m	GD
"	15.9.18	"	Enemy shell arrived about B.H.Q. during the morning. Our aircraft very active all day. A prisoner (wounded) from a young German soldier of 5 Coy, two lines, at different times in the morning. A Batt was sent down to Brigade. Relief carried out and handed over.	GD
"	16.9.18	"	Quiet night. Orders received to move back into the support line. We were relieved by 12. 15th Batt at some Regt. and the relief was carried out successfully. Batt H.Q. were at N.21.b.3. & M.14.92. and forward H.Q. at N.9.c.7.2. 2/Lt. W.S.A. Gillett arrived open to take over command of the Battalion	GD
"	17.9.18	"	Strong shelling of advanced H.Q. by M.G. & M.13 but fortunately no casualties were sustained.	GD
"	18.9.18	"	After a quiet night there was occasional shelling by the enemy during the day. Fatigue & wire parties were sent out under the Coy arrangements.	GD
"	19.9.18	"	Orders were received to proceed to Front line, and take above the D.L.I. Gt Batt moved off by Companies. "C" Coy & "D" and the relief was successfully carried out. Battn. Q. & still at N. M.17c central. M.R.36 S.W.1. G.D.	GD
"	20.9.18	"	Hostile shelling by the enemy during the early hours of the morning. With fine but still humid weather. Our artillery very active during the day increasing towards evening.	GD

CONFIDENTIAL

Army Form C. 2118.

September 1918.
11th Batt. Somerset Light Infantry.

WAR DIARY
or
INTELLIGENCE SUMMARY.
(Erase heading not required.)

Instructions regarding War Diaries and Intelligence Summaries are contained in F.S. Regs., Part II. and the Staff Manual respectively. Title pages will be prepared in manuscript.

Place	Date	Hour	Summary of Events and Information	Remarks and references to Appendices
TRENCHES.	21.9.18	All day	The Enemy shelled us rather heavily, especially between the hours of 12.10 a.m and 4 a.m. Four patrols went out during the night to locate some suspected Enemy Machine Gun posts, but it was found that there were no posts established, but the enemy seemed to patrol from shell hole to shell hole.	AUBERS 36 S.W.4 G.D
"	22.9.18	"	On the AUBERS ridge to our right front a considerable amount of enemy movement could be seen. Hostile shelling again was pretty hot. We were relieved during the night by the R.S.F. and fortunately during this tour we had no casualties.	G.D
BOUT DEVILLE.	23.9.18	"	We took up our new Billets and Batt. H.Q. was established at BOUT DEVILLE. The Companies were between PONT DUHEM and ROUGE CROIX.	G.D
"	24.9.18	"	The Battalion went to the Baths at RIEZ BAILLEUL.	G.D
"	25.9.18	"	General training started 9 o'c. a.m.	G.D
"	26.9.18	"	General training starts 9 a.m. The enemy shelled us with Gas & H.E. shells, and three of our men were sent to the A.D.S. slightly gassed.	G.D
"	27.9.18	"	The Colonel inspected all Head Quarter Staff in full marching order.	G.D
"	28.9.18	"	General training.	G.D
"	29.9.18	"	This day, being Sunday, the Padre held a Church Parade at 9.30 at H.Q., a Voluntary service was held for A. Coy at 4:30 p.m. and B, C & D Coy at 6:30 p.m. at the Recreation Room.	G.D
"	30.9.18	"	General training carried on. The Colonel inspected B & C. Coys in full marching order. The Boche continued shelling of the neighbourhood at intervals.	G.D

W. Mansfield
Lt. Col.
Commanding 11th Batt. Somerset L.I.

CONFIDENTIAL
OCTOBER 1918
11th Batt Somerset L.I.

ORIGINAL
Army Form C. 2118.

WAR DIARY
or
INTELLIGENCE SUMMARY.
(Erase heading not required.)

Instructions regarding War Diaries and Intelligence Summaries are contained in F.S. Regs., Part II. and the Staff Manual respectively. Title pages will be prepared in manuscript.

Place	Date	Hour	Summary of Events and Information	Remarks and references to Appendices
BOUT de VILLE	1.10.18	14.00	The Battalion moved to CHARTER HOUSE POST Nº B6a7.8.6. During the night the enemy heavily shelled our position.	MAP REF. SHEET 36 1/40,000
CHARTER HOUSE POST	2.10.18	All day	Ordinary trench routine with 'D' Company. The shelling by the enemy had abated during the night.	
"	3.10.18	"	The Batt travelled by motor lorries to ROUGE de BOUT Sh. 36 NW G 20.18.6. Bomb attacks and shell fire at 14.30 to FLEURBAIX where the Batt billets to have tea. During the enemy shelled with trench mortar and blew three candles. At 18.30 moved on and established in HQ at FERRETS POST HQ Build. Advanced HQ was est. at HQ 25.32 and the Batt. proceeded to relieve the BERKSHIRE REGT in the front line.	
TRENCHES	4.10.18	"	A & D bombers in front line. B & C bombers in support. Heavy shelling by the enemy. Advanced HQ moved forward to SHAFTESBURY AVENUE L.19.c.6.8.	
"	5.10.18	"	Advanced HQ heavily shelled by enemy.	
"	6.10.18	"	A company attempted to advance with the object of securing a wood but were met by great opposition and had to retire. Lieut ... again bombarded enemy. Some prisoners taken. B.C. going out. Fort Hall and A & D in support. 2nd Lt Mason and 2nd Lt Plate Pl A & B to this observers D.p... Wounded. ... Divisional General visits the line. 2nd battalion line at L.19.a.6.2. 'C' company moves forward several units the line.	
"	7.10.18	"	Enemy shelling billets till of advanced HQ.	
"	8.10.18	"	Enemy shelling village till 13.015. CREIER. C. Company advances 500 yds. B Company advances our post.	
"	9.10.18	"	Very quiet all day until 12.00 when enemy starts shelling.	
"	10.10.18	"	Quiet day. The Batt. was relieved by the 1st DUKE OF WELLINGTON R.L. relief 18.30 + 22.00 + took the Batt relief was successfully carried out with the Batt. marched back to billets at H9 c 25.7. In FLEURBAIX	
FLEURBAIX	11.10.18	"	This day was spent in cleaning up and resting.	
"	12.10.18	"	The Batt. went to baths by companies and the Lt Coll'ns continues training.	
"	13.10.18	"	Church Parade was ordered for 09.30 but owing to inclement weather was cancelled.	

CONFIDENTIAL
Army Form C. 2118.
ORIGINAL

OCTOBER
11 Batt. Somerset Light Infy.

WAR DIARY
or
INTELLIGENCE SUMMARY.
(Erase heading not required.)

Instructions regarding War Diaries and Intelligence Summaries are contained in F.S. Regs., Part II. and the Staff Manual respectively. Title pages will be prepared in manuscript.

Place	Date	Hour	Summary of Events and Information	Remarks and references to Appendices
FLEURBAIX	14.10.18	All day	The Batt. attended a Brigade commanders Conference held at the Bde. headquarters for the purpose of forming a model attack. Stands 266587 2/8 Stalmeg NE of the Military huts.	
"	15.10.18		The Batt. carried on the programme of training for the day.	
"	16.10.18	14.00	The Batt. received orders during the morning to move forward to BOIS GRENIER, and moved off at 14.00 arriving about 17.00, staying for the night	MAP REF. SHEET 36
BOIS GRENIER	17.10.18	All day	The Batt. moved further forward by road to PERENCHIES arriving about 18.00, and went into Billets for the night	40,000
PERENCHIES AND MARQUETTE	18.10.18	All day	The Batt. moved from PERENCHIES by road to MARQUETTE arriving about 16.00 Billets were attained for the Batt. but later orders were received to advance on to MONS EN BAROEUL and the Batt. moved off at 20.15 arriving at their destination about 23.00 where they occupied Billets for the night.	
MONS en BAROEUL	19.10.18	"	The Batt. starts by road for L'HEMPONPONT at 12.00 arriving about 16.00. Billets were there occupied for the night	
L'HEMPONPONT	20.10.18	"	The Batt. left at 16.50 for WILLEMS arriving about 19.00. Billets were taken for the night.	
WILLEMS	21.10.18	"	The Batt. stood by awaiting orders to move. No order was received this day so that spent in refitting and cleaning up.	

Confidential
Army Form C. 2118.
ORIGINAL

OCTOBER 1918
11th Batt Somerset Light Infantry
WAR DIARY or INTELLIGENCE SUMMARY
(Erase heading not required.)

Instructions regarding War Diaries and Intelligence Summaries are contained in F. S. Regs., Part II. and the Staff Manual respectively. Title pages will be prepared in manuscript.

Place	Date	Hour	Summary of Events and Information	Remarks and references to Appendices
WILLEMS	22-10-18	All day	The Batt. moved off at 11.00 to EPINETTE there to relieve the 14th Batt Royal Sussex Regim. the front line. Dinner was served at TEMPLEUVE at 13.00 and the Batt. moved off at 14.00 arriving about 15.00. Steady progress was established at H.28.b.30. and the relief was successfully carried out. The enemy's rearguard ceased his bombardment decided to hold it's line of the ruins of SCAUT Lingwardly.	MAP REF. SHEET No 34 1/40,000
FRONT LINE	23-10-18	"	Batt. HQ were advanced to H.29.a.08. Enemy centres by B & C who's headquarters were then established at H.23.c.98. The intr Batt Boundary being an runs from 2nd Lieut I.20 until 15 ghed then I.14.d.00 enemy artillery was active. A shell struck a house used as a HQ by C Co. at I.25.a.b.b. unfortunately causing the following casualties. The deceased men were buried in the churchyard at REMEGNIES - CHIN.	✓
"	24.10.18	"	Enemy artillery again very active and the area round Batt. HQ was shelled, but no casualties sustained. O. Ptrg went out from Co. across the river ESCAUT and captured an enemy light M.G. returning without sustaining any casualties. The Patrol was under the direction of 2/Lt J.A. Proctor who had under his command 11 following of 2/Lt Downs &. L/C. Blackell. H., L/C. Hammerton E. & Pte. Newman J.C., Pte. Hinchliffe S., Pte. Stevens E.A., Pte. Burkett J.A., Pte. Lambert H.W., Pte. Miller C.E. The Brigadier visited Batt. HQ and congratulated 2/Lt Proctor on the exploit.	✓

CONFIDENTIAL
Army Form C. 2118.
ORIGINAL

OCTOBER 1918
11th Batt Somerset Light Infantry

WAR DIARY
or
INTELLIGENCE SUMMARY.
(Erase heading not required.)

Instructions regarding War Diaries and Intelligence Summaries are contained in F. S. Regs., Part II. and the Staff Manual respectively. Title pages will be prepared in manuscript.

Place	Date	Hour	Summary of Events and Information	Remarks and references to Appendices
FRONT LINE	25.10.18	all day	During the early morning enemy artillery was active. A.Co. changes with C.Co. positions	
			of the two platoons in the front line. A Patrol sent out by A.C. to reconnoitre the	MAP. REF.
			EAST side of the river ESCAUT returned an enemy light M.G. and four prisoners	SHEET 34
			(1 Corporal & 3 men) The Patrol was under the direction of Lt. O-C. Later R.H. Ridler	1/40,000
			and was in charge of 2/Lt. O.W. Jenkins who was with him the following O.R. 2/L	
			James E.J. O/11 Cpl C.H. 4Cpl Broussard H. Pl. B. 2/L H. Pl. 3rd HE. Cl. Johnson W.	
			Cl. Jarrett H.B. Cl. Foot B.G. Cl. Goodhurst A. Cl. Lawrence J. Cl. Dolly G. Cl. Dean O.	
			The same evening a covering party was sent out to cover a party of Engineers	
			who were to build a foot bridge across the river. This party consisted of the following M.G.	
			Part but after about two hours 1 4 5 Platoons all were comfortable withdrawn owing	
			to hostile T.M. & M.G. fire. The party was under the direction of Sgt. Bounfords A. all	
			the following : Cpl. Thomas W. Cpl. Rollo O.S. Cpl. Howlis A.B. Cpl. Bromley T. Cpl.	
			[illeg] Cpl. Reeves F.G. Cpl. Robinson W. Cpl. Elias J. Cpl. Jarvis A.F.	
			Commander of — ×	
26.10.18	all day	Enemy artillery quiet. Cl. Bull was relieved by 11. & 15 Batt Durham Reg the relief started at 1600	
			and was carried out successfully. Bns were taken over from the Town Royk HULLAND	
			and the Batt. places in support × The Brigadier wrote endorsing congratulating	
			the Batt. on the success of the Operations which	
			results in valuable identifications being secured	

CONFIDENTIAL

Army Form C. 2118.

ORIGINAL

OCTOBER 1918
11th Batt Somerset Light Infantry

WAR DIARY
or
INTELLIGENCE SUMMARY.
(Erase heading not required.)

Instructions regarding War Diaries and Intelligence Summaries are contained in F.S. Regs., Part II. and the Staff Manual respectively. Title pages will be prepared in manuscript.

Place	Date	Hour	Summary of Events and Information	Remarks and references to Appendices
HOLLAIN	27.10.18	All day	The day was spent in resting and cleaning after leaving the front line. A voluntary service was held by the Chaplain at 18.00.	
	28.10.18		Programme of training was carried out by all & mechanics during the afternoon. Stomache bars given over to sports, football matches being 10 lg s and other suitable games.	MAP REF. SHEET 37 1/10,000
	29.10.18		Training continues under somewhat arrangement. Some of the different companies were watching and showing the articles of clothing which were left at the Quartermasters Stores.	
	30.10.18		The morning was occupied with the usual programme of training. Orders were received to move forward to relieve the 7/10 Durhams in the front line. The Batt. moved off at 15.30 the relief being completed at 21.40. Batt. H.Q. was established at the CHATEAU E19 b.4. D Coy was placed in the Outpost line with H.Q. at T14.a.9.3. A & B Coys were Right and Left of post (in reserve). C Coy in reserve. The roads & tracks were heavily shelled by the enemy during the relief, and the vicinity of H.Q. was also shelled during the night. B Coy bath/bothie was damaged and two D Co. men wounded by T.M's there being the only casualties sustained during the relief.	
FRONT LINE	31.10.18		Conditions unchanged. Enemy artillery showed much reduced activity until 13.30 after which hour roads & tracks used by us were again intermittently bombarded. Our artillery did its usual vigorously. 2nd Lt. J. Brown was unfortunately KILLED by a sniper this day. He was buried in the Churchyard at RAMEGNIES - CHIN. The Chaplain officiating at the graveside.	

M Lundgfield Lt/Col
Commanding
11th Bn Somerset Light Infantry

11th Bn Somerset L.I. November 1915

WAR DIARY
INTELLIGENCE SUMMARY

Place	Date	Hour	Summary of Events and Information	Remarks and references to Appendices
ESQUELMES	1/11/18		From Nine Enemy Artillery been active especially on wood surrounding Batt. H.Q. Operation Orders were sent for a raid on CABARET LIETARD Dug a. Gterwood by A Coy. Batt. H.Q. & Gun [group] moved forward at 22.00 hrs to D Coy H.Q.	
	2/11/18		The raid on Cabaret Lietard was successful one light-machine gun & 6 enemy O.R. being captured. Unfortunately the garrison being killed. The advance commenced at 04.00 hrs being preceded by an Artillery & M.G. Barrage for 5 minutes. The villag[e] being entirely cleared by the Enemy. A Company relieved at 05.30 hrs. Enemy Artillery shelled Batt. H.Q. area Entire casualties were sustained. Our forward positions were also shelled intermittently during the day.	
	3/11/18		Enemy Artillery again very active. During morning operation orders were issued for a Patrol to reconnoitre CABARET LIETARD. Toute of Reply was supplied by B Coy.	
	4/11/18			

11th Bn. SOM L.I. NOVEMBER 1918

WAR DIARY

INTELLIGENCE SUMMARY

(2) Confidential

Place	Date	Hour	Summary of Events and Information	Remarks and references to Appendices
ESQUELMES	3/11/18		The Patrol advanced at 0300 hrs after several barrage by Artillery & M.G. The outskirts of the village of CATZ ARETT LIE 7ARD was secured but no signs of the enemy found & the Patrol withdrew at 0430 hrs. A further patrol was sent out under Capt. Hook at 0500 hrs & returned at 0620 hrs reporting that they had advanced as far as the Railway without seeing any signs of the enemy. A civilian returned stated that the enemy had left the village & were got through to BREGAL & then when orders were subsequently received, two more patrols under Lieut CABARET LIE MARD & Lieut SKILLYN, fire were sent forward in order to occupy the village. A Coy advanced between these 2 patrols & they were pushed forward but persisted out & to met with heavy M.G. fire from the houses in the village & were compelled to retire. Enemy had only two more planes that afternoon returned to Old CABARET LIE MARD until M. 5. C Coy were sent forward in support of A Coy & occupied that end running across the north loop of the R. Bend of the river.	DAR

1/1/78th Som. L.I. NOVEMBER 1918.

Army Form C. 2118.

WAR DIARY
or
INTELLIGENCE SUMMARY.
(Erase heading not required.)

(3) Gofdenhul

Place	Date	Hour	Summary of Events and Information	Remarks and references to Appendices
ESQUELMES	6/11/18		A Coy having sustained numerous casualties + being exposed to the adverse weather conditions, having partially been relieved by B. Coy at 0500hrs. The Enemy Artillery & MGs were extremely active all day against Honnasey fue being extremely directed on transverse tracks leading to our bridges across the ESCAUT. The Battalion was relieved by the 1/5th Bn ESSEX REGT. Relief commencing at 1600hrs & being completed by 2100hrs.	
HULANS	6/11/18	1900	The Bn. H.Q. reopened at HULANS at the hour the Bn greeted their former billets here being placed in Brigade Reserve.	DATE
"	7/11/18		The day was spent in refitting & general cleaning up. Kits were inspected & deficiencies made good as far as possible.	DATE
"	8/11/18		Orders were received for the Battalion to move to TOUFFLERS and the march commenced at 1600hrs.	DATE
TOUFFLERS	"		The Battalion arrived tired & soaked in TOUFFLERS	DATE

11th Bn. Som. L.I.

NOVEMBER 1915.

Army Form C. 2118.

(4) Confidential

WAR DIARY
INTELLIGENCE SUMMARY.
(Erase heading not required.)

Place	Date	Hour	Summary of Events and Information	Remarks and references to Appendices
TOUFFLERS	9/11/15		The day was spent in copying out the necessary reorganisation of the Battalion, cleaning up of kit, etc.	D.A.B.
	10/11/15		Orders were received to move to QUHTREVENTS. Battalion moved off at 06.15 hrs. owing however, the difficulty of transport over the River ESCAUT was decided by B.Brigade that Battn. or detatchmt. be billets were taken in the neighbourhood of PECQ.	D.A.B.
PECQ	11/11/16		+ TRIEU DE WASMES. The day was spent in carrying out the normal training programme.	
	12/11/16		ditto	D.A.B.
	13/11/16		ditto	D.A.B.
	14/11/16		ditto	D.A.B.
	15/11/15 12.01		The Battalion moved off to CHERENG whither billets were obtained for the night.	D.A.B.
CHERENG	14/11/15 05.30		The Battalion moved off to SECLIN (10 klms S. of LILLE)	D.A.B.

1/11th Bn. Som. L.I.

NOVEMBER 1916

Army Form C. 2118.

WAR DIARY
or
INTELLIGENCE SUMMARY. (5) (continued)

Place	Date	Hour	Summary of Events and Information	Remarks and references to Appendices
SECLIN	17/11/18		The day was spent in carrying out the weekly reorganisation of the Battalion, resting, refitting, cleaning billets.	
"	18/11/18		Training was resumed. Special attention being paid to Ceremonial & Educational Scheme.	D.A.F.S.
"	19/11/18		The day was spent in carrying out the Training Programme.	D.A.F.S.
"	20/11/18		ditto	D.A.F.S.
"	21/11/18		ditto	D.A.F.S.
"	22/11/18		Billets were inspected by the Brigade Commander at 10.00 hrs.	D.A.F.S.
"	23/11/18		The day was spent in Ceremonial Educational & Recreational Training.	D.A.F.S.
"	24/11/18		ditto	D.A.F.S.
"	25/11/18		ditto	D.A.F.S.
"	26/11/18		ditto	D.A.F.S.
"	27/11/18		ditto	D.A.F.S.
"	28/11/18		ditto	D.A.F.S.

11th Bn "L.I." · NOVEMBER 1916

Army Form C. 2118.

WAR DIARY
INTELLIGENCE SUMMARY
(Erase heading not required.)

Confidential

Place	Date	Hour	Summary of Events and Information	Remarks and references to Appendices
SECLIN	29/11/18		A Battalion concert was held in the old German Cinema Hall at 18.00 hrs. Arranged & organized by Revd W.C. CAMPLING C.F.	APPS
"	30/11/18		The day was spent in carrying out the usual training programme	APPS

H.Henry Major
O.C. 11th Bn. L.I.

Orderly Room 30 NOV 1918 11th Bn. Somerset L.I.

11th Bn Somerset L.I.   December 1918.

WAR DIARY
or
INTELLIGENCE SUMMARY.

Army Form C. 2118.

(1) Confidential

Place	Date	Hour	Summary of Events and Information	Remarks and references to Appendices
SECLIN	1/12/18		The usual training programme was carried out. An Officers Mess for Officers of the whole Battalion instituted.	
"	2/12/18		Training carried out as usual	
"	3/12/18		ditto	
"	4/12/18		ditto	
"	5/12/18	1000h	Orders received for the Battalion to move to NOEUX LES MINES. Battalion Embussed & proceeded to NOEUX LES MINES passing through LENS & the old front line on the way.	
NOEUX LES MINES	"	1400	On arrival every endeavour was made to find out the huts allotted for billeting the Battalion, one hut sufficient C. Coy. Talk of a start in another Camp	

H. Henry Major
Commanding 11th Battalion Somerset L.I. (T.F.)

1t/4 Bn Som. L. I. December 1918.

Army Form C. 2118.

WAR DIARY
INTELLIGENCE SUMMARY
(2) Confidential

(Erase heading not required.)

Place	Date	Hour	Summary of Events and Information	Remarks and references to Appendices
NOEUX LES MINES	9/12/18		Parties sent out to discover derelict dumps. A section of R.E. sent from Brigade to take down Nissen huts & re-erect them in the Camp. DAPR	
	7/12/18		Educational Training recommences. C. Coy returns to camp. on 2/Lt D.L.I. take over huts in which they were billetted. DAPS	
	8/12/18		Brigade Service held. After the service the Divisional General Major Genl. presented Ribbons to Lt. Refojada, 2/Lt O.W. Jenkins a 2/Lt B rown awarded M.C. for open hinsin. Lt S. Chelot. B. Plt. Burrows awarded a bar to his M.M. A/Cpl Cox L/Cpl Bemond Plt Henman awarded the M.M.	DAPR

17th Bn. Somerset L.I.
ORDERLY ROOM
31 DEC 1918

WAR DIARY
INTELLIGENCE SUMMARY

11th Bn Som. L.I. — December 1915
Captain J. Col

Place	Date	Hour	Summary of Events and Information	Remarks and references to Appendices
No E UK LES MINES	9/12/18		The usual Training Programme carried out	
"	10/12/18		A class in Horsemanship for Officers held under Lt. Armstrong. Transport Officer. Battalion Lewis Guns inspected by Lewis Gun Officer.	
"	11/12/18		A Battalion route march took place in the morning. A. Coy & B. HQ went to 13 others in afternoon. The Battalion continued its Programme of training during the day.	offs. sts.
"	12/12/18			offs. sts.
"	13/12/18			offs. sts.
"	14/12/18			offs. sts.
"	15/12/18		The Battalion attended Church Parade at 9 AM. B.W. the remainder of the day kept for rest	offs.

11th BATT. SOM.L.I.

WAR DIARY
or
INTELLIGENCE SUMMARY.
(Erase heading not required.)

Army Form C. 2118.
DECEMBER 1918
(CONFIDENTIAL)

Place	Date	Hour	Summary of Events and Information	Remarks and references to Appendices
HOEDIC-LES-MINES	21/12/18	—	The Batt. carried out its usual Training Programme each day	
"	22/12/18	—	The Batt. attended Church Parade at G.H.Q. Hut, the remainder of the day being spent at rest.	
"	23 + 24/12/18	—	The Batt. carried out its usual Training Programme each day	
"	25/12/18	—	Christmas Day. Special Dinners were provided for Officers & other Ranks & the Battalion attended Church Parade at G.H.Q. Hut. The remainder of the day was spent in various amusements. The weather being stormy. No was observed as a Holiday, only the ordinary routine work being carried on.	
"	26/12/18	—	The Battalion carried out its usual programme of Work & Education. The Batt. Baths were allotted to the Battn. from 13.30 to 16.30hs.	
"	27/11/18	"	The usual programme of Work & Education were carried out. Owing to inclement weather no Battn. Assemble Parade could be held.	
"	28/12/18	"	The Batt. attended Church Parade at Y.M.C.A Hut. The remainder of the day being spent at rest.	
"	29/12/18	"	Education Classes & Work Parties as usual.	
"	30/12/18	"	The Batt. carried out a programme of Musketry on details. Two conferences in the morning on the ordinary ambitions and one in the afternoon. Practice 9.10 was carried out by Platoons.	

H. Henry
Major
Commanding 11th Battalion Somerset L.I. (T.F.)

Confidential.

1/5th Somerset Light Infantry

Army Form C. 2118.

WAR DIARY
or
INTELLIGENCE SUMMARY.
(Erase heading not required.)

Jan. 1919

Place	Date	Hour	Summary of Events and Information	Remarks and references to Appendices
Noeux-les-Mines	1st and 2nd	all day	The battalion carried out its usual programme of work and education; the afternoon being devoted to sport.	
	3rd.	all day.	The battalion carried out its usual programme of work and education; the afternoon being devoted to sport. 10 other ranks left the battalion for demobilisation.	
	4th	all day	The battalion carried out its usual programme of work and education; the afternoon being devoted to sport.	
	5th	all day	The battalion marched by companies (owing to bad weather) to the Y.M.C.A. for Divine Service. The association match against the divl. R.E. postponed owing to bad weather.	
	6th	all day.	Usual programme of work and education was carried out, with sport in the afternoon.	
	7th	all day	Musketry was arranged and cancelled by Brigade so the usual programme was carried out.	
	8th.	all day.	Route March in the morning; foot inspection in the afternoon.	
	9th	all day	The battalion carried out its usual programme of work and education; the afternoon being devoted to sport.	10 P. Sheet

1/ Somerset Light Infantry. Confidential.

Army Form C. 2118.

WAR DIARY
or
INTELLIGENCE SUMMARY.
(Erase heading not required.)

JAN. 1919

Instructions regarding War Diaries and Intelligence Summaries are contained in F.S. Regs., Part II and the Staff Manual respectively. Title pages will be prepared in manuscript.

Place	Date	Hour	Summary of Events and Information	Remarks and references to Appendices
Noeux-les-Mines	10th	all day	The battalion carried out its usual program of work and education; the afternoon being devoted to sport.	
	11th	do.	ditto	
	12th		The battalion attended Church Parade at Y.M.C.A. Hut.	
	13th		The battalion received orders to move to Abancourt. The afternoon and evening were spent on station loading transport etc.	
	14th		The train finally left Noeux-les-Mines at 0130 hours, and the rest of the day was spent on the train. "B" Coy were detrained at Abbeville, where they were to-day. Train arrived at Abancourt 1930 hours, and the night was spent on the train.	
Abancourt	15th		Companies marched up to the camp and spent the remainder of the day in making themselves comfortable.	
	16th		The day was spent in preparing for our new work, which is the staffing of a camp to accommodate drafts of men on their way to & from England for demobilization things.	W.W.J.M. Oakes 2/Lt
	17th		ditto	ditto
	18th		ditto	ditto

11 Bn. Somerset. L. Inf.   Confidential.

Army Form C. 2118.

WAR DIARY
or
INTELLIGENCE SUMMARY.
(Erase heading not required.)

JAN. 1919

Place	Date	Hour	Summary of Events and Information	Remarks and references to Appendices
ABANCOURT.	19th	all day	The battalion paraded at 0930 for C.of E. service in Abancourt Cinema.	
	20th	"	The day was spent in doing fatigues and education	
	21st	"	ditto	
	22nd	"	The King's Colour was presented to the battalion by Maj. Gen. Smyth V.C. G.O.C. 59th Division. Lieut. Nelmes was officer in charge of Colour Party.	
	23rd	"	The day was spent in doing fatigues and education	
	24th	"	At 0430 hours, the first party of 1100 Australians arrived at the staging camp as reinforcements.	
	25th	"	The day was spent in work at the staging camp & other routine duties	
	26th	"	The Battalion attended Church Parade at 09-30 hours	
	27th	"	The day was spent in carrying out the usual Routine Programme	
	28th	"	ditto	
	29th	"	ditto	
	30th	"	ditto	
	31st	"	ditto	

Cont'd.
11th Bn. Somerset Light Infy.

WAR DIARY
INTELLIGENCE SUMMARY

Army Form C. 2118.

1st SOM. L.I. FEB 1919

Place	Date	Hour	Summary of Events and Information	Remarks and references to Appendices
BLARGIES	1/2/19	ALL DAY	The Bn.tt. carried out its usual Routine Programme	
ABANCOURT AREA	2/2/19	"	ditto	
	3/2/19	"	ditto	
	4/2/19	"	ditto	
	5/2/19	"	ditto	
	6/2/19	"	At 14.30 hrs. 1 Officer and 50 O.R. arrived & left Blargies for ABANCOURT ABBEVILLE (Marching Company) Train will full Equipment ABANCOURT AREA. The remainder of the Battalion carried out its usual Routine Programme.	
	7/2/19	"	At 14.30 hrs. the remaining Officers and O.R. of "A" 3 "B" marched to ABANCOURT Station, entrained there at 15.12 hours for ABBEVILLE. The remainder of the Battalion carried out its usual Routine Programme.	
	8/2/19	"	The Battalion carried out its usual Routine Programme of the day	
	9/2/19	"	ditto	
	10/2/19	"	ditto	
	11/2/19	"	ditto	
	12/2/19	"	ditto	

11th SOM.L.I. WAR DIARY (2.)

FEB. 1919

Army Form C. 2118.

INTELLIGENCE SUMMARY.

CONFIDENTIAL.

(Erase heading not required.)

Place	Date	Hour	Summary of Events and Information	Remarks and references to Appendices
BLARGIES (RBANCOURT to AREA	1/3/2/19	All day	The Battalion carried out its usual Routine Programme for today.	
	25/2/19	"	2 Officers and 178 O.R. arrived as Reinforcements from the 6th R.F. The remainder of the Battalion carried out its usual routine programme for the day.	
	26/2/19	"	The Battalion carried out its usual routine programme for today.	
	27/2/19 28/2/19	"	Hqts. Headqus. & 12 I.R. moved to NEUFCHATEL where lifts are to be arranged for 2 Squadrons of the R.A.F. The remainder of the Battalion carried out its usual routine programme for the day.	

Robert Hill
E.C.J.
Commdg. 11th Bn Som.L.I.

11TH SOMERSET. L.I.

MARCH. 1919

WAR DIARY
or
INTELLIGENCE SUMMARY.
(Erase heading not required.)

Army Form C. 2118.

Place	Date	Hour	Summary of Events and Information	Remarks and references to Appendices
ABANCOURT	1-3-19	all day	The Battalion carried out its usual Routine Programme for the Day.	
	2-3-19	11.00	The Billetting Party under Lt Hawkins returned from NEUFCHATEL.	
		all day	The Battalion carried out its usual Routine Programme for the Day.	
	3-3-19		Under orders received from Commandant ABANCOURT AREA the Battalion moved quarters, to staging camp being replaced in former quarters by 18th Bn MIDDLESEX. (Evening) Lt Hithes & 2nd Lt Withy, Sansom & Palmer proceeded to CALAIS unless orders received from Commandant ABANCOURT AREA.	
	4-3-19	09.00	The C.O. inspected "D" Coy & "B" Coy Reinforcements	
		all day	The remainder of the Battalion carried out its usual Routine Programme for the Day	
	5-3-19	09.00	The C.O. inspected H.Q Personnel	
		10.00	The C.O. inspected "C" Coy and "A" Coy Re-inforcements	
		12.00	The C.O. inspected Transport	
			Orders were received from Commandant Abancourt Area for the Battalion to proceed to CALAIS on 7.3.19	
	6-3-19	all day	The day was spent in packing and making preparations for the move to CALAIS. The Battn. on relief by the C.O.W. Man Cuddoss Bade farewell to Command Maj. H. Morton Edwards	
	7-3-19	13.00	The Battalion entrained for CALAIS, the train leaving at 13.55 see Annex	
CALAIS	8-3-19	00.20	The train arrived at Fontinette Station CALAIS. Breakfast was served on the train and the Battalion detrained at 0700 hours marching to COULOGNE Camp where quarters were furnished	

11TH SOMERSET L.I.

WAR DIARY
or
INTELLIGENCE SUMMARY.
(Erase heading not required.)

Army Form C. 2118.

MARCH 1919.

CONFIDENTIAL

Place	Date	Hour	Summary of Events and Information	Remarks and references to Appendices
COLOGNE	9.3.19	all day	The Battalion spent the day in cleaning & fitting up the Bks. which was in a very dirty condition.	
		23.30	Warned by Staff Capt. to have an Officer detailed at once to accompany another Staff Officer to British Prison where have a disturbance was threatened. Lt Harris detailed also to be ready to detail 200 men to proceed to the Prison at short notice.	JM
CALAIS.	10.3.19	0050	Lt Harris returned with orders (verbal) for 200 men to proceed to the Prison by 0330 hours. 100 from "C" Coy, 100 men of "D" Coy, detailed also 2 Lt Dugan Schults, Hawkins & Lt Webb.	
		0315	Party mounted at 0315; tea & biscuits served. Party told off as a Company moved off at 0445 hours. Lt Harris in Command.	
		0910	Field Kitchen with Breakfast moved off at 0910 hours.	
		11.45	All Quiet Reported at 11.45 hrs.	
		18.00	Detachment relieved at 1800 hours by Party of 15th Essex Regt.	JM
	11.3.19	0430	Further Party of 5 Offrs & 200 Marks proceeded to British Prison to relieve the Essex Regt under the Command of Lt Harris MC Bronsall.	
		0900	"D" Coy on the party on being relieved by 25.K.R.R proceeded to VENDREUX Camp being joined there by remainder of Coy from COLOGNE Camp.	
		20.00	98 of the Re-inforcements from 1st Batt. Som L.I. moved from VENDREUX to COLOGNE Barracks and went down on the Strength of their Unit.	
	21.03		Orders were received for further party to proceed to Bristol Camp tomorrow 12-3-19	JM
	12.3.19	06.00	3 Offrs & 100 O.R reported to O.C. Troops VENDREUX to relieve 25.K.R.R on guard at the 7 Military Prison.	
		17.30	3 Offrs & 100 O.R. proceeded to the 7 Military Hospital to relieve Guard, mounted at 06.00 hours.	JM

11th Somerset L.I.   March 1919   Army Form C. 2118.

WAR DIARY
or
INTELLIGENCE SUMMARY.   CONFIDENTIAL
(Erase heading not required.)

Place	Date	Hour	Summary of Events and Information	Remarks and references to Appendices
COULOGNE (CALAIS)	13.3.19	AM	The Battalion carried out its routine Programme for this day	
	14.3.19	do	ditto	
	15.3.19	do	ditto	
	16.3.19	do	ditto	
	17.3.19	do	ditto	
	18.3.19	do	ditto	
	19.3.19	do	Reinforcements of 6 Officers & 242 O.R. arrived from the 7th Gen. Bn. 2.6. & were taken on the strength. The remainder of the Battalion carried out its routine Programme for the day	
	20.3.19	do	The Battalion carried out its routine Programme for the day	
	21.3.19	do	ditto	
	22.3.19	do	ditto	
	23.3.19	do	ditto	
	24.3.19	do	ditto	
	25.3.19	do	ditto	
	26.3.19	do	ditto	
	27.3.19	do	ditto	
	28.3.19	do	ditto	
	28.3.19	12.00	Lt. Col. A.V.S. Pattern D.S.O. relinquished duty and assumed command of the Battn. Major F. Musey relinquished command of the Battn. carried on its Routine programme for the day	
	29.3.19	AM	The Battalion carried out its routine programme for the day	
	30.3.19	do	ditto	
	31.3.19		The Battn. carried out its routine programme for the day	

A.V.S. Pattern Lt. Col.
Commdg. 11th Bn. Som. L.I.

11th Br. Somerset Light Infantry   April 1919   Army Form C. 2118.

WAR DIARY
or
INTELLIGENCE SUMMARY.
(Erase heading not required.)

(Confidential)

Place	Date	Hour	Summary of Events and Information	Remarks and references to Appendices
COURCAGE (CALAIS)	1/4/19	Allday	Major H. Hussey temporarily placed in command of No 5 Bisons of War Corp. The Battalion carried out its routine programme for the day.	
Coulogne	2/4/19	Allday	Detachment from Abbeville consisting of 6 officers (2/Lt G.W. Hoole in command) and 109 other Ranks arrived to day. The remainder of the Battn carried out its routine programme for the day.	
Coulogne	3/4/19	Allday	The Battalion carried out its routine programme for the day.	
Coulogne	4/4/19	Allday	Reinforcements consists of 48 other Ranks arrived from 1st Bn Somerset L.I. Remainder of Battn carried out its routine programme for the day.	
Coulogne	5/4/19	Allday	Battalion carried out its Routine Programme for the day. ditto	
Coulogne	6/4/19	ditto	ditto	
Coulogne	7/4/19	all day	JELLALABAD DAY. Anniversary was observed. First Communion of service to the commemorated as parade of No 5 Platoon of No 4 Coy took Retalin celebrated Jellalabad Day. Toasts to officers drunk at B.Cr. Coy Mess in the evening.	
Coulogne	8/4/19	allday	Battn carried out its routine programme for the day.	
Coulogne	9/4/19	ditto	ditto	
Coulogne	10/4/19	ditto	ditto	
"	11/4/19	ditto	ditto	
"	12/4/19	ditto	ditto	
"	13/4/19	ditto	ditto	
"	14/4/19	ditto	ditto	

1/1 Batt. Somerset Lgt Infy K Hawkins

WAR DIARY
or
INTELLIGENCE SUMMARY
(Erase heading not required.)

Army Form C. 2118.

April 1919

(Confidential)

Place	Date	Hour	Summary of Events and Information	Remarks and references to Appendices
Cologne Calais	15/4/19	Midday	Reinforcements consisting of 37 o/ranks reported for 6 Bn. Somerset L.I. Remainder of Batts. carried out its routine programme for the day.	
"	16/4/19	"	The Battalion carried out its routine programme for the day.	
"	17/4/19	"	ditto	
"	18/4/19	"	Good Friday. As far as duties would permit this day was observed as a Holiday.	
"	19/4/19	"	The Battalion carried out its routine programme for its day	
"	20/4/19	"	Easter Sunday. ditto	
"	21/4/19	"	Easter Monday. As far as duties would permit this day was observed as a Holiday.	
"	22/4/19	"	The Batt. carried out its routine programme for the day.	
"	23/4/19	"	ditto	
"	24/4/19	"	Battalion routine at training of Personnel inspected by Brigadier Gen. C.H.L. James C.B. C.M.G. G.O.C. 173 Infantry Brigade	
"	25/4/19	"	Batt. carried out its routine programme for the day.	
"	26/4/19	"	ditto	
"	27/4/19	"	Battn. Church Parade inspected by Major Gen. not signed. G.O.C. 59 Div.	
"	28/4/19	"	Batt. carried out its routine programme for the day.	
"	29/4/19	"	ditto	
"	30/4/19	"	ditto 2/185	

K. Hawkins Capt Lt Col.
Commandy 1/18 Som L.I.

11th Bn Somerset Light Infantry Confidential

Army Form C. 2118.

WAR DIARY
or
INTELLIGENCE SUMMARY.

(Erase heading not required.)

Place	Date	Hour	Summary of Events and Information	Remarks and references to Appendices
Boulogne (Calais)	From 16/5/19 to 31/5/19		May 1919. The Battalion carried out the routine programme each day throughout the month.	

H. Hussey Major
Comdg. 11th Bn Somerset L.I.

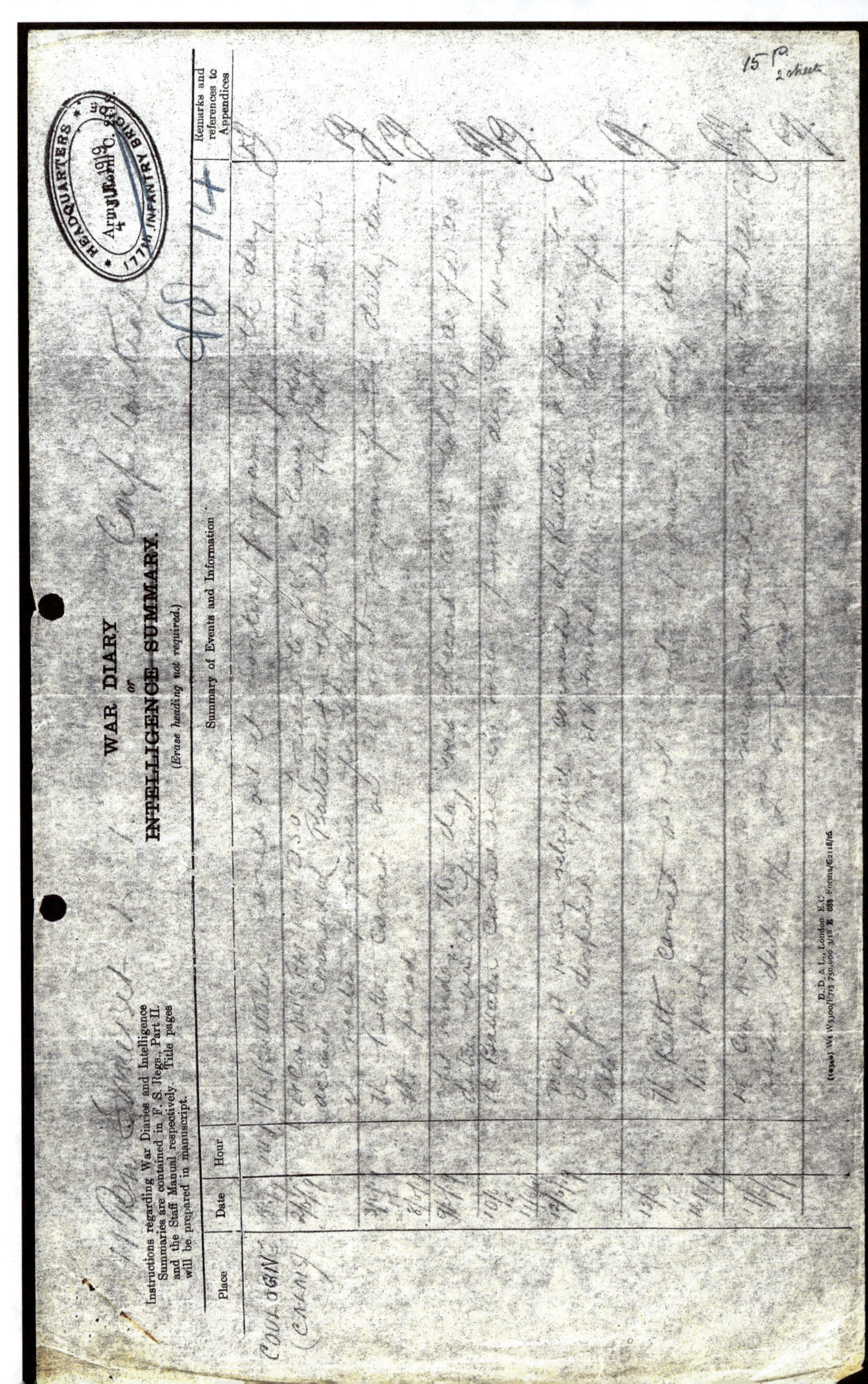

1/1 Bn Somerset L.I.   Confidential

Army Form C. 2118.

WAR DIARY
or
INTELLIGENCE SUMMARY.
(Erase heading not required.)

Place	Date	Hour	Summary of Events and Information	Remarks and references to Appendices
Colaba Bombay (India)	10/4/19 to 27/4/19		The Battalion carried on its routine program duty during this period.	
	19/4/19		This day arranged to be held as a special holiday in celebration of the resumption of the armistice agreed upon by the Peace Terms has been agreed upon by the enemy. Arrangements were arranged at field including cricket, running, other games etc.	
	27/4/19		The Battalion turned out to route march & firing in tactical manner & present.	

M. Frankin Major
for Lt Col.
Commanding 1/1 Bn Som L.I.

144th Inf. Bde.

CONFIDENTIAL

Army Form C. 2118.

WAR DIARY
or
INTELLIGENCE SUMMARY.

(Erase heading not required.)

July 1919

11th Somerset L.I.

Place	Date	Hour	Summary of Events and Information	Remarks and references to Appendices
COULOGNE	1/13		The Battalion carried out its routine duties during this period.	
CALAIS	14		Monday being the British National Fete day was observed as a holiday, no fatigues or parades were carried out.	
	15/18		The Battalion carried out its routine duties and so spent the period.	
	19		Two days being this day appointed for the British National Rejoicings a celebration of that was observed as a holiday.	
	20/31		The Battalion carried out its routine duties during this period.	

1. 8. 19

A.S. Parkman
Comdg. 11th Bn Somerset L. Infantry
Lt. Col.

Confidential. Army Form C. 2118.

WAR DIARY
or
INTELLIGENCE SUMMARY.

11th Bn Somerset L.I.

AUGUST 1919.

Place	Date	Hour	Summary of Events and Information	Remarks and references to Appendices
COULOGNE CALAIS.	1/8/19	2.15	O.R.S. Having been warned for probable embarkation to EGYPT and BLACK SEA left for duty. Liable to U.K. duty.	
	2/8/19		O.R.S. ditto	
	3/8/19		The remainder of the Battalion carried out no routine programme during this period. Also having been warned the Battalion to concentrate received "A" and "D" Companies proceeded this day	
	5/8/19		BEAUMARAIS from VENDROUX and took up their new quarters at WINCHESTER CAMP "B" and "C" Companies + H.Q. proceeded their new quarters also at WINCHESTER and took up CAMP.	
BEAUMARAIS CALAIS	7/8/19 to 31/8/19		The Battalion carried out no routine during this period. A Nominal Roll was prepared of personnel wyn...	

Commanding 11th Bn S.L.I.

TERRITORIAL FORCE ASSOCIATION.

County of Somerset.

County Territorial Hall,
Taunton.
5th December 1922.

Major-General Sir Henry Everett, K.C.M.G., C.B.

I now send you a short history of the 11th Battalion, which has been supplied by the Officer late Commanding.

Paragraph 1. "The Battalion was raised in the Spring of 1918.

The Battalion, then the South Western Brigade Battalion was raised in April 1915.
What is meant, I think, is that the Battalion was re-organized and renamed in the Spring of 1918.
You already have particulars of the early life of the Battalion.

Paragraph 2. "Garrison Guard (T.F.) Battalion".

I have not seen this designation used before, and think it must be an unofficial, local, one, and that the real description was "Garrison Battalion".

Sd. F.Kennedy,
Major,
Secretary, Somerset T.A.Assn.

SHORT HISTORY OF THE 11th SOMERSET LIGHT INFANTRY.

The Battalion was raised in the Spring of 1918 and after training at Wrentham, Suffolk, proceeded to France on the 7th May 1918.

The Battalion was originally formed for Garrison duty and was known as a Garrison Guard (T.F.) Battalion. The men composing it were at first mainly of B.1 category and in June 1918 the Battalion was employed chiefly in digging and training in the neighbourhood of VIELFORT WOOD.

Whilst the Commander-in-Chief fully recognised the men's physical limitations the Battalion was in fact called upon to play the rôle of a fighting unit and early in August 1918 occupied the front line trenches south of ARRAS.

From that time onwards the Battalion was treated as troops of an A.1 category would be and was called upon to carry out similar duties in the fighting line as an A.1 Battalion. A special letter of praise on the way in which the Battalion fulfilled its duties and stating they would henceforth not be referred to as a B Category Battalion owing to the good work they had done was received from the Corps Commander in October 1918.

About mid August of 1918 the Battalion as part of the 177th Brigade, 59th Division, went into the sector east of ST. VENANT and ROBECQ south of the FOREST OF NIEPPE and fought continuously up to the Armistice along the line of advance ST. VENANT - CALONNE - LESTREM - LA GORGUE - LAVENTIE - FLEURBAIX - BOIS,GRENIER-WEZ, MACQUART - PERENCHIES - LILLE - WILLEMS - TEMPLEUVE - OBIGIES (River Scheldt north of TOURNAI).

A short diary of the places and dates is annexed hereto. Both when engaged in front of the AUBERS RIDGE and particularly during operations on the Scheldt the Battalion carried out some very successful minor tactical operations and were several times congratulated (see copy of Memoranda from the Brigade dated 26th October 1918 and 2nd November 1918 attached hereto).

Ultimately the Battalion was the first in the Division to obtain a bridge head across the Scheldt in the neighbourhood of OBIGIES and the Division were actually crossing through the bridge head so obtained by the Battalion when the Armistice occurred.

After the Armistice the Battalion was reinforced by large drafts of men from the 1st, 6th and 7th Battalions and was employed at policing dumps, depots and prisons in France until the summer of 1919 when it was disbanded.

11th SOMERSET LIGHT INFANTRY.

Short Diary of Events.

1918.

September	17th.	At PONT DU HEM on LA BASSÉE road.
"	19th.	In outpost line in front of LAVENTIE.
"	22nd.	In reserve at BOUT DE VILLE.
"	27th.	In outpost line by FAUQUISSART.
October	3rd.	Battalion moved through FLEURBAIX to BOIS GRENIER and took over outpost line from outgoing Division.
"	6th.	Battalion reconnoitre in force a small wood under ridge by PETIT MARAIS.
"	9th.	Still in outpost line by GRAND MARAIS farm.
"	11th.	In reserve at FLEURBAIX.
"	16th.	Battalion moved up to BOIS GRENIER.
"	17th.	Moved through WEZ MACQUART to PERENCHES.
"	18th.	To MARQUETTE via VERTFEUILLE and same night through north of LILLE to MONS EN BAROEUL.
"	19th.	Moved to L'HEMBONPONT.
"	20th.	To WILLEMS.
"	22nd.	Took over outpost line on Scheldt in front of RAMEGNIES CHIN. The Battalion floated a raft and got patrols across the river.
"	25th.	Battalion make raid across Scheldt and capture 4 prisoners of 7th Bavarian I.R. and machine gun.
"	26th.	Battalion in reserve at HULANS.
"	30th.	Battalion again take over outpost line on Scheldt in front of ESQUELMS.
November	1st.	Battalion heavily engaged all day. (Night of 1st/2nd Battalion cross the Scheldt and raid small village of CABRIOLET LIETARD and capture prisoners and gun).
"	5th.	Battalion engaged in heavy fighting all day in order to secure bridge head of CBARIOLET LIETARD. Position secured towards evening and formed bridge head for Division.
"	7th.	At HULANS in reserve.
"	8th.	Moved to TOUFFLEURS.

November 10th.   Moved up to cross Scheldt but are ordered to billets in PECQ.

"   11th.   Armistice.

R/14/320, dated 26/10/18.

Headquarters,
177th Infantry Brigade.

      The Brigadier wishes me to convey to you his congratulations on the very successful patrol enterprise carried last night which resulted in the capture of four prisoners and a machine gun. The identification obtained was most valuable.

      He considers that the whole affair reflects great credit on the 11th Somerset L.I. and in particular on 2/Lt.Jenkins and 12 other ranks who carried out the operation.

      He hopes that O.C., 11th Somerset L.I. will see his way to afford special indulgencies while they are in reserve to all ranks who took part.

(Sd/-) B.H.Robertson,
Captain,
B.M., 177th Infantry Brigade.

R.14/351.

Headquarters,
177th Infantry Brigade.

      The Brigadier wishes his heartiest congratulations to be conveyed to Lt-Col.Gillett and all ranks of 11th Somerset L.I. and particularly to "A" Company under Captain Ridler, on the most successful raid carried out last night. The operation was a very difficult one, and he considers that the results obtained do great credit to the Battalion.

      He is glad to note that for the purposes of successful raids, it is a matter of indifference to 11th Somerset L.I. which section of the line they are holding.

      He wishes also to thank the 296th Bde. R.F.A. for the excellent artillery support provided.

Sd/- B.H.Robertson,
Captain,
B.M., 177th Infantry Brifade.

2nd November 1918.

www.ingramcontent.com/pod-product-compliance
Lightning Source LLC
Chambersburg PA
CBHW081449160426
43193CB00013B/2426